CW01655208

THE DEVIL WITHIN

EVIL IN OUR WORLD TODAY

Wendy Sheffield

Spiritwriterspeaks

Order of publications by Wendy Sheffield

Spirit Writer: A Journey of Spiritual Awakening and Self-Discovery
(Books 1-4)

Series of spiritual books published in 2024
The Devil Within: Evil In This World Today
Spirit Writer: This Journey Called Life
Spirit Writer: The Spirit Guide Connection
Spirit Writer: The Enigma of the Spirit World

This book is published by SPIRITWRITERSPEAKS

A CIP record for this book is available from the British Library.

To my spirit guides who guide me towards the light,
may they keep this light shining so that I know
the way!

I am but a messenger for their many messages...

Credit: ilbusca

‘The Devil Within’ Epigraph

Only by recognising and embracing our inner demons can we truly conquer them and unleash our full potential.

* * *

True self-awareness comes from recognising and confronting the devil within us, for only then can we truly rise above our own darkness.

* * *

The growth begins when we have the courage to acknowledge and confront our own inner demons, for it is only by recognising our devil within that we can truly overcome it.

* * *

The growth begins when you confront and acknowledge the devil within, for only then can you conquer your own darkness and find the strength to ignite your inner light.

* * *

Only when you acknowledge the darkness within can you truly embrace the light.

* * *

Contents

Introduction

'True power lies not in avoiding or ignoring evil, but in the ability to comprehend, challenge and ultimately conquer it'

The main objective of this book is not to empower the devil or evil, but rather to assist individuals in recognising their existence in today's world and empowering themselves against them.

While some individuals may be apprehensive about reading a book on the subject of the devil and evil, avoiding such literature will not eliminate one's perception of these forces. Those who are more enlightened will understand that being aware of both sides of the coin equips them better for the battle between good and evil. Indeed, knowledge ultimately leads to empowerment!

Across history, humanity has been captivated by the concept of evil and the presence of a malevolent entity. From ancient myths to religious texts, the devil has been portrayed as a force immersed in darkness, enticing mankind towards sin and suffering.

In our contemporary society, scholarly minds, theologians, and skeptics continue to grapple with questions surrounding the existence of the devil. This book delves into this intriguing topic by drawing upon various religious texts, philosophical discussions, and psychological theories.

Prepare yourself for an engaging exploration of evil as we delve into an insightful analysis of the enduring influence and presence of the devil in our lives today.

* * *

Part 1

Let's Begin

Chapter 1

Knowledge is Power

'Knowledge is the key that unlocks the door to endless possibilities and empowers us to shape our own destiny'

Why is it important to understand the concept of the devil and the existence of evil? Knowledge is Power!'

Firstly, it provides us with insights into the nature of good and the existence of righteousness. By exploring the darker side of humanity and acknowledging the presence of evil forces, we gain a deeper understanding of what it means to be virtuous and moral. Knowing about the devil and evil serves as a contrast to goodness, allowing us to appreciate the values and qualities that are opposite to evil, such as compassion, empathy, and kindness.

Secondly, knowledge about the devil and evil helps us navigate and make sense of the often complex and challenging aspects of life. By recognising the existence of evil, we become better equipped to identify and confront it in our own lives and society. This awareness empowers us to make informed choices, stand up against injustice, and work towards creating a better world.

Furthermore, studying the devil and evil facilitates personal growth and self-reflection. It prompts us to question our own actions, motivations, and beliefs, thus aiding in our moral and spiritual development. By delving into the nature of evil, we become more self-aware and strive to align our actions with our values, enabling us to live a more meaningful and purposeful life.

Lastly, understanding the devil and evil is essential for religious and theological perspectives. Many religious traditions consider the devil as a symbol of temptation and the embodiment of evil. Knowledge about the devil and evil allows believers to engage with their faith more deeply, examining how their religious teachings address evil and how they can overcome its influence.

* * *

In conclusion, learning about the devil and evil provides us with a comprehensive world view that encompasses both good and bad. It helps us define and uphold moral values, navigate the challenges of life, foster personal growth, and deepen our religious understanding. By acknowledging and understanding the darker aspects of existence, we can strive to create a more just, compassionate, and harmonious world.

* * *

Chapter 2

The different faces of the devil & evil

'Evil comes in many disguises, but its true face is always destruction'

Some say the devil is merely a figure of folklore, a product of our collective imagination. Others argue that evil forces are alive and well, manifesting in the darkest that lurks within humanity.

To explore this further, let's examine the signs of the devil's presence in our world.

Deception

First, we have deception. How often do we encounter lies, manipulation, and dishonesty in our daily lives? Where does this dark energy come from? We witness it in politics, in business, even in personal relationships. Could these actions be influenced by an evil force, silently working to divide and conquer humanity?

Cruelty

Then there's cruelty. Look at the violence, the wars, the hatred that plagues our world. It's difficult to believe that man is totally responsible for all the cruelty in the world.

Is the devil real?

The devil, if real, thrives in the chaos caused by our worst impulses. It preys on our weaknesses, amplifying them, and turning them into monstrous acts.

Remember, where there is evil there is love, kindness and compassion - choose your path wisely!

But here's the thing, every act of evil also gives birth to countless acts of love, kindness and compassion. It's within each one of us to choose which path we take.

The battle between good and evil exists within each of us. It's a daily struggle, fought in the depths of our hearts and minds.

Does the devil exist in our world today?

So, does the devil exist in our world today? Perhaps, but to defeat it, we must acknowledge our own capacity for darkness and actively choose the light.

Remember, it's not about defeating some external entity, but rather, it's about the battle within ourselves - the battle to be the driving force of love and compassion in a world that desperately needs it.

* * *

Chapter 3

The concept of evil

'Evil does not define humanity, it challenges us to rise above and choose the path of compassion and righteousness'

In order to understand the devil's role in our modern world, it is crucial to delve into the complex and elusive concept of evil. Throughout history, philosophers, theologians, and psychologists have grappled with defining evil, often coming up with varying interpretations and theories.

Religious standpoint

From a religious standpoint, evil is often seen as the absence of goodness and a result of the devil's influence. However, secular perspectives challenge this notion, asserting that evil is a human construct rooted in individual and societal beliefs.

Psychologist's standpoint

Psychologists analyse evil through the lens of human behaviour, exploring the dark side of the human psyche that can lead to harmful actions. They consider factors such as moral development, societal influences, and psychopathy.

Examine the different definitions and perspectives on evil

By examining the different definitions and perspectives on evil, we can gain a deeper understanding of the devil's role in our modern world. We have provided a terminology section at the end of this book to explain words in our world today.

* * *

In the next chapter, we will explore the portrayal of the devil across various religious traditions and cultural contexts, shedding light on the multifaceted nature of evil.

* * *

Chapter 4

Portrayal across cultures & religions

'Across cultures and religions, the portrayal of the devil and evil reminds us that darkness exists in different forms, but it is our choice whether to succumb to it or rise above, embracing the light within'

Now that we have explored the various definitions and interpretations of evil, it is important to examine how the devil is portrayed in different cultures and religious traditions. By examining these different cultural and religious perspectives on the devil, we can gain a broader understanding of how evil is conceptualised and the role it plays in shaping our modern world. Fuller accounts are in Part 3 of this book.

Ancient Mythology

In ancient mythology, figures such as Loki in Norse mythology are mentioned.

Egyptian mythology

Egyptian mythology personifies chaos, deceit, and destruction.

Christianity

While the devil is a prominent figure in Christianity, other religions have their own versions of a malevolent being that embodies evil.

Judaism

In Judaism, the concept of the devil and evil holds great significance in the Jewish community. It serves as a reminder for individuals to resist temptation and choose the path of righteousness. By understanding the complexities of evil, individuals can better navigate life and make choices that align with their beliefs and values. The concept of the devil and evil is an integral part of Jewish theology and shapes the beliefs and practices of Judaism.

Hinduism

In Hinduism, there is the concept of Asuras, powerful supernatural beings who represent chaos and oppose the divine order.

Buddhism

In Buddhism, Mara is seen as a tempter and embodiment of desire, leading individuals astray from enlightenment.

Islam

In Islam, the devil, known as Iblis or Shaytan, plays a significant role in tempting and misleading humans away from the righteous path.

* * *

In the next chapter, we will explore the implications of the devil's existence and influence on our society today.

* * *

Chapter 5

Does evil exist in our modern world?

'In a world filled with both light and darkness, acknowledging the existence of evil is not a sign of weakness, but rather a call to rise above it with even greater compassion and strength'

Now that we have delved into the various interpretations of the devil across cultures and religions, it is crucial to analyse the presence of evil in our modern world. While our perception of evil may have evolved over time, its existence continues to shape our society, whether we believe in the devil or not.

One need only turn on the news or scroll through social media to be confronted with stories of violence, corruption, and injustice. From acts of terrorism to systemic racism, the manifestations of evil are all around us.

Evil can be found not only in grand-scale atrocities but also in the more subtle forms that permeate our everyday lives. It's present in the small acts of cruelty, the dishonesty that erodes trust, and the apathy that allows suffering to persist.

Understanding the prevalence and influence of evil in our modern world is essential if we are to combat it effectively.

* * *

In the following chapters, we will examine the ways in which evil impacts our lives and explore strategies for promoting goodness and justice in a world seemingly consumed by darkness.

* * *

Chapter 6

A symbol of temptation & immoral behaviour

'Within the depths of temptation lies the devil's playground, enticing us with immoral choices that challenge the purity of our souls'

Throughout history, the devil has been portrayed as a symbol of temptation and immoral behaviour. Regardless of one's belief in the literal existence of the devil, the concept serves as a cautionary tale and a representation of the darker aspects of human nature.

In modern society, we are constantly confronted with various temptations and opportunities to engage in immoral behaviour. It could be as simple as cheating on a test, succumbing to materialistic desires, or engaging in harmful gossip. These seemingly insignificant choices may not invoke the grandiose image we often associate with the devil, but they contribute to the propagation of evil in our world.

Recognising the devil's role as a symbol allows us to be more aware of our own actions and the potential impact they can have on ourselves and others. By making conscious choices rooted in integrity and empathy, we can work towards minimising the influence of evil in our lives.

* * *

In the following chapter, we will explore how individuals can resist temptation and make choices aligned with goodness and morality, thereby taking an active role in combating evil in our modern world.

* * *

Chapter 7

Personal choice & responsibility

'Your personal choices and actions define your path in life, and the responsibility lies solely on you to create a journey worth living'

In the face of temptation and immoral behaviour, it is ultimately up to each individual to make conscious choices that align with goodness and morality. The role of personal choice and responsibility cannot be overstated when it comes to combating evil in our modern world.

Resisting temptation requires a strong sense of self-awareness and a willingness to confront our own weaknesses. It is crucial to recognise that every choice we make has consequences, both for ourselves and for others. By taking ownership of our actions and decisions, we take an active role in shaping a more compassionate and just society.

It is also important to remember that no one is immune to temptation. We are all fallible beings, and it is through acknowledging our own vulnerabilities that we can better understand and empathise with others who may succumb to temptation. By showing compassion and offering support to those who have made mistakes, we can strive to uplift one another and create a more forgiving and understanding community.

* * *

In the next chapter, we will delve deeper into specific strategies and techniques that individuals can adopt to resist temptation and contribute to the eradication of evil in our modern world.

* * *

Chapter 8

Good and evil - The ultimate relationship

'Within the delicate dance of good and evil lies the ultimate test of our humanity, for it is in our choices that we reveal our true nature'

In order to fully understand the role of evil in our modern world, it is essential to examine the relationship between good and evil. Throughout human history, these two forces have been intertwined, sometimes conflicting and other times coexisting harmoniously.

The concept of moral relativism

One way to approach this examination is to consider the concept of moral relativism. Moral relativism suggests that what is considered good and evil is subjective and varies from person to person, culture to culture. This perspective acknowledges that there may not be a universal standard for determining what is morally right or wrong.

However, it is important to note that this does not mean that anything goes or that we should abandon all ethics and values. Rather, it highlights the need for open-mindedness and empathy towards differing viewpoints. It also emphasises the importance of critical thinking and evaluating actions and decisions based on their consequences and impact on others.

* * *

By exploring the relationship between good and evil, we can gain a deeper understanding of the complexities surrounding morality in our modern world. This understanding, in turn, can inform our own personal choices and contribute to the collective effort in combating evil and promoting goodness.

* * *

Chapter 9

Understand & confront evil

'True power lies not in avoiding or ignoring evil, but in the ability to comprehend, challenge and ultimately conquer it'

Examining the existence of evil in our modern world is not simply an intellectual exercise; it has real-life implications for each and every one of us. Understanding and confronting evil is a vital aspect of personal growth and self-awareness.

By acknowledging the existence of evil, we are able to better recognise and address its presence in our own lives. This requires us to examine our own actions and choices, and to take responsibility for the impact we have on others. It also involves developing a moral compass that guides us towards making virtuous decisions.

Confronting evil means actively opposing its influence and working towards creating a more just and compassionate society. This can involve standing up against injustice, advocating for the oppressed, and promoting positive change. It also means cultivating qualities such as empathy, kindness, and forgiveness.

* * *

In grappling with the role of evil in our lives, we become more resilient, compassionate, and enlightened individuals. Ultimately, it is through this understanding and confrontation of evil that we sow the seeds of a better world for ourselves and future generations.

* * *

Chapter 10

The devil and evil throughout time

'Evil is merely the manifestation of the devil's silent whispers; it is up to us to discern its disguise and choose the path of righteousness'

Throughout history, the concept of evil and the devil has been a prevalent theme in various cultures and societies. From ancient mythologies to modern literature and films, the portrayal of evil forces has captivated the human imagination. These representations of darkness and malevolence serve as a reminder of the constant battle between good and evil.

* * *

In ancient mythologies, we see the existence of evil entities taking the form of demons, monsters, and dark gods. For example, in Greek mythology, figures like Hades, the god of the underworld, and Medusa, a cursed creature with snakes for hair, represent the embodiment of evil. These tales were meant to caution individuals about the consequences of immoral behaviour and the dangers of succumbing to temptation.

Religious texts also extensively discuss the idea of evil and the devil. In Christianity, Satan is depicted as a fallen angel who rebelled against God and tempts humanity to sin. The story of Adam and Eve in the Bible's Book of Genesis is a testament to the devil's ability to corrupt the innocence of mankind. This notion of evil serves to emphasise the importance of resisting temptation and following a righteous path.

In more recent times, the portrayal of evil has taken various forms in literature and popular culture. Classic literary works like Bram Stoker's "Dracula" and Mary Shelley's "Frankenstein" delve into the darker aspects of human nature and explore the consequences of pursuing forbidden knowledge. These stories tap into our deepest fears and desires, forcing us to confront our own capacity for evil.

Moreover, modern films and television series often depict villains who personify evil. From Darth Vader in the "Star Wars" franchise to the Joker in "The Dark Knight," these characters exhibit a twisted moral compass and evoke a sense of fear and fascination in audiences. The existence of these villains not only adds depth and conflict to the narrative but also allows viewers to reflect on the nature of good and evil in the real world.

* * *

In conclusion, the concept of evil and the devil has permeated human culture throughout time. Whether rooted in ancient mythology, religious texts, or contemporary literature, the existence of evil forces serves as a reminder of the eternal battle between good and evil. Through exploring these representations, we gain a better understanding of our own moral compass and the challenges we face in maintaining a harmonious society.

* * *

Part 2

Portrayal of the devil and evil in our world today

Amidst the spectrum of beliefs about the existence of the devil and evil, scholars, theologians, and skeptics serve as guiding compasses to navigate the depths of faith, reason, and doubt.

Chapter 1

The devil & evil in psychological theories

'In understanding the devil and evil, we delve into the depths of the human psyche, where darkness lurks, and where the battle between good and evil takes shape'

This chapter explores the fascinating topic of the devil's role in our society, drawing on psychological theories.

Throughout history, the concept of evil and the presence of a devil figure has captivated the minds of individuals across different cultures and societies. From ancient religious texts to modern psychological theories, the existence and influence of evil have been examined and debated. In this chapter, we will explore the psychological theories surrounding the devil and evil and their significance in understanding human behaviour.

Sigmund Freud's theory of the human psyche

One of the most influential psychological theories regarding evil is Sigmund Freud's theory of the human psyche. Freud believed that evil or the devil represented the dark, irrational side of human nature that existed within every individual. He theorised that the human psyche was composed of three components: the id, ego, and superego. The id represented our basic primitive instincts and desires, often associated with evil or selfish behaviour. The ego acted as the mediator between the id and the superego, which represented our moral conscience. According to Freud, the devil or evil was a product of the id overpowering the superego, resulting in immoral and destructive behaviour.

Carl Jung's theory of the collective unconscious

Another psychological theory that explores the concept of evil is Carl Jung's theory of the collective unconscious. Jung proposed that the collective unconscious was a shared reservoir of inherited knowledge and experiences that influenced an individual's thoughts and behaviours. Within the collective unconscious, Jung suggested the existence of archetypes, which are universal symbols or images that represent common themes or patterns of human existence. The shadow archetype, according to Jung, represents the darker aspects of human nature, including evil and the devil. He believed that by acknowledging and integrating our shadow, we could achieve personal growth and individuation.

In addition to these individual theories, social psychology has also explored the phenomenon of evil within the context of group behaviour.

Stanley Milgram's famous obedience experiments

Stanley Milgram's famous obedience experiments highlighted the capacity for individuals to commit harmful actions under the influence of authority figures. The studies demonstrated that under certain circumstances, ordinary individuals could engage in acts of extreme cruelty, illustrating the potential for evil within the human psyche.

However, it is important to note that psychological theories surrounding evil and the devil are not universally accepted, and many criticisms have been raised against them. Some argue that these theories oversimplify complex human behaviours and fail to consider the role of socio-cultural factors in influencing individual thought and action. Others believe that evil is a religious or philosophical concept that cannot be adequately explained through psychological theories.

In conclusion, the devil and evil have long fascinated human beings, and psychological theories have sought to shed light on their existence and influence. Whether through Freud's theory of the human psyche,

Jung's concept of the collective unconscious, or social psychology's examination of group behaviour, these theories provide insights into the dark aspects of human nature. However, it is important to approach these theories with a critical lens, recognising their limitations and considering alternative perspectives when understanding the complexity of human behaviour.

* * *

Chapter 2

Views of scholars

This chapter explores the fascinating topic of the devil's role in our society, drawing on views of scholars.

* * *

In today's world, the concept of evil and the devil is often viewed differently by scholars and intellectuals. While some may dismiss the idea of the devil as merely a superstition or myth, others argue that evil exists in various forms and is a fundamental part of human nature.

Devil and evil is a product of religious beliefs and cultural conditioning

One perspective on the devil and evil is that it is purely a product of religious beliefs and cultural conditioning. Many scholars argue that the idea of the devil was created by religious institutions to control and manipulate people. They believe that evil is not an external force, but rather a manifestation of human actions and choices.

Societal structures and individual behaviour

From this viewpoint, evil is seen as a result of societal structures and individual behaviour. Poverty, inequality, greed, and power dynamics are all seen as contributing factors to evil deeds. Scholars argue that by addressing these root causes and promoting social justice, we can reduce the occurrence of evil in our world.

Evil is a universal force that exists independently of human beliefs and actions

On the other hand, there are those who believe that evil is a universal force that exists independently of human beliefs and actions. They argue that evil cannot simply be reduced to societal factors, but rather has a metaphysical dimension. These scholars see evil as a fundamental aspect of human nature, rooted in our capacity for selfishness, cruelty, and destruction.

From this perspective, the devil is seen as a symbol of this underlying evil in the world. It represents the temptation and the allure of destructive behaviours and actions. These scholars argue that by understanding the true nature of evil and acknowledging its presence, we can better resist its influence and work towards building a more compassionate and just society.

Regardless of the perspective one takes, it is clear that evil is a complex and multifaceted concept. Whether it is seen as a religious symbol or as a reflection of human nature, the existence of evil cannot be denied. Acknowledging its presence and working towards its eradication is a collective responsibility shared by individuals, communities, and societies.

* * *

In conclusion, the scholars' view of the devil and evil in our world today varies widely. Some see evil as a construct of religious institutions, while others see it as a fundamental aspect of human nature. Regardless of the perspective, the recognition and understanding of evil is crucial in tackling its manifestations and striving for a better and more just world.

* * *

Chapter 3
Views of theologians

This chapter explores the fascinating topic of the devil's role in our society, drawing on views of theologians.

* * *

Throughout history, theologians from various religious traditions have had differing views on the concept of the devil and evil. The devil, often seen as a malevolent being with supernatural powers, has been portrayed differently in different religious texts and teachings.

In Christianity, the devil is believed to be a fallen angel who rebelled against God. According to Christian theology, he is the epitome of evil and tempts humans to sin. Some theologians view the devil as a literal entity, a personal force of evil that actively works against God's plan. Others, however, interpret the devil as a symbol of the darker aspects of human nature, representing the struggles and temptations that individuals face in their pursuit of goodness and righteousness.

In Islamic theology, the devil is known as Shaytan. According to the Quran, Shaytan was once a righteous jinn who disobeyed God's command to bow before Adam. Similar to Christianity, Islamic theology portrays Shaytan as a tempter who seeks to mislead humans and lead them astray from God's path. Some theologians interpret Shaytan as a metaphor for internal psychological struggles, emphasising the importance of self-discipline and resisting evil temptations.

In Hinduism, the concept of evil is not personified in the same way as in Christianity and Islam. Hindu theology suggests that evil is a result of ignorance and spiritual imbalance. The nature of evil is seen as more complex, with different gods and goddesses representing both positive and negative aspects. Evil is viewed as a temporary aspect of existence that is ultimately overcome through spiritual growth and enlightenment.

Buddhism, on the other hand, does not attribute the existence of evil to any external force or being. Instead, Buddhism teaches that suffering and evil are inherent parts of the human condition, resulting from attachment and ignorance. The path to liberation from suffering lies in overcoming these afflictions through wisdom and compassion.

It is important to note that these are broad generalisations, and within each religious tradition, there are variations in beliefs and interpretations. Furthermore, theologians within the same tradition may hold different views on the nature of evil and its origins. These sections are further explored in Part 3 of this book.

* * *

In conclusion, the views of theologians on the devil and evil vary across different religious traditions. While some portray the devil as a literal entity, others view it as a metaphor or symbol representing the negative aspects of human nature. Similarly, the concept of evil itself differs in each tradition, ranging from a personal force of temptation to an inherent aspect of existence. Understanding these diverse perspectives can enrich our understanding of the complex relationship between good and evil in the world.

* * *

Chapter 4

Views of skeptics

This chapter explores the fascinating topic of the devil's role in our society, drawing on views of skeptics.

* * *

Skeptics have always held a unique perspective on the existence of the devil and evil in our world today. While many people believe in the existence of supernatural entities that represent evil, skeptics argue that such beliefs are simply a product of human imagination and religious indoctrination.

To skeptics, the concept of the devil is nothing more than a myth created by ancient civilisations to explain the unexplainable. They argue that throughout history, humans have always sought to find meaning in the world around them, and attributing natural disasters or human suffering to the work of a supernatural being such as the devil provided a convenient explanation. Skeptics believe that as our understanding of the world has evolved and scientific knowledge has increased, there is no longer a need for such myths and superstitions to explain the presence of evil.

Furthermore, skeptics point out that the belief in the devil often leads to a culture of fear and religious fanaticism. They argue that people who believe in the existence of the devil often see evil in every corner and attribute every negative occurrence to the influence of this supernatural entity. This can lead to a narrow-minded and paranoid worldview, where individuals are constantly searching for signs of the devil's presence and engaging in witch hunts or witch trials.

Skeptics also question why, if the devil is indeed real, he has not been proven to exist scientifically. They argue that if the devil truly exists and has the power to wreak havoc in our world, there should be some tangible evidence to support this claim. However, skeptics argue that there is no empirical evidence to support the existence of the devil or any other supernatural entity, and therefore, it is more reasonable to assume that evil is a product of human actions and societal circumstances.

* * *

In conclusion, skeptics provide a thought-provoking perspective on the existence of the devil and evil in our world today. While many people may find comfort in the belief that there is a supernatural force behind the evils of the world, skeptics argue that such beliefs are simply a product of human imagination and religious indoctrination. They emphasise the importance of critical thinking and empirical evidence when examining the existence of supernatural entities, and encourage individuals to question long-held beliefs and superstitions.

* * *

Chapter 5

The devil & evil in Philosophical Discussions

'The greatest trick the devil ever pulled was convincing the world that evil exists only on the outside, when in reality, it resides within the depths of our minds'

This chapter explores the fascinating topic of the devil's role in our society, drawing on philosophical discussions.

The concept of evil has been a topic of philosophical discussions for centuries. It is a complex and controversial subject, often associated with the presence of a supernatural entity known as "the devil." Throughout history, various philosophers have grappled with the nature and existence of evil, attempting to provide explanations and theories that shed light on this dark aspect of human experience.

One prominent philosophical perspective on evil is found in the works of religious thinkers. Many religious traditions, such as Christianity, Islam, and Judaism, posit the existence of a malevolent being known as the devil or Satan. According to these beliefs, evil originates from this supernatural figure and manifests itself in the world through human actions. Evil is seen as a force that seduces individuals into engaging in immoral behaviour and corrupts their souls.

However, not all philosophical discussions about evil involve the supernatural. In fact, many philosophers approach evil from a secular perspective, seeking to understand it in purely human terms. These thinkers often trace evil back to human nature, exploring the motivations, desires, and actions that lead individuals to commit harmful acts. Some argue that evil arises from a combination of factors, such as ignorance, selfishness, and a lack of empathy for others.

Friedrich Nietzsche

One influential philosopher who grappled with the problem of evil from a secular standpoint was Friedrich Nietzsche. He believed that evil was not an inherent characteristic of individuals, but rather a product of social and cultural influences. Nietzsche saw morality as a human invention that was often used to suppress and control individuals, leading to the emergence of ressentiment – a feeling of resentment and hostility that stems from a sense of powerlessness. According to Nietzsche, this ressentiment could give rise to evil actions when individuals seek to assert themselves against those they perceive as oppressors.

Contemporary discussions

In contemporary discussions, the concept of evil continues to be a source of debate among philosophers. Some argue that evil is an objective reality, while others contend that it is subjective and dependent on individual perspectives and cultural norms. Additionally, there are those who reject the idea of evil altogether, suggesting that it is an outdated and unnecessary concept that no longer holds explanatory power in understanding human behaviour.

* * *

In conclusion, discussions about evil in philosophy encompass a wide range of perspectives and theories. Whether approached from a religious or secular viewpoint, the nature and existence of evil continue to be explored and debated by philosophers seeking to understand this dark aspect of human experience.

Chapter 6

Modern literature and films

In more recent times, the portrayal of evil has taken various forms in literature and popular culture.

Classic literally works

Bram Stoker's "Dracula" and Mary Shelley's "Frankenstein" delve into the darker aspects of human nature and explore the consequences of pursuing forbidden knowledge. These stories tap into our deepest fears and desires, forcing us to confront our own capacity for evil.

Modern films and television series

Modern films and television series often depict villains who personify evil. From Darth Vader in the "Star Wars" franchise to the Joker in "The Dark Knight," these characters exhibit a twisted moral compass and evoke a sense of fear and fascination in audiences. The existence of these villains not only adds depth and conflict to the narrative but also allows viewers to reflect on the nature of good and evil in the real world.

* * *

Chapter 7

Spiritual messages about the devil & evil

'The devil exists not only in our fears, but in the choices we make. It is our responsibility to embrace our inner light and defy the darkness, for evil has no power over a soul guided by love and truth'

* * *

'Darkness cannot drive out darkness, only light can do that. Hate cannot drive out hate, only love can do that'

Martin Luther King, Jr.

* * *

'In the darkest corners of our souls, the devil can whisper his deceitful messages, but it is in the light of our spirituality that we find the strength to resist and conquer evil'

* * *

'In a world overcome by darkness, remember that the devil's greatest fear is your light, for it has the power to dispel even the darkest shadows'

* * *

'The greatest weapon against the devil and evil is not fear or ignorance, but the unwavering power of love and faith'

* * *

Chapter 8

Witchcraft & demonology quotes

Definition of Witchcraft: The practice of magic arts using potions, unguents, powders, sacrifices, and blood to cast spells and gain favours with the help of evil spirits. Witches are female and warlocks are considered male. On their "Sabbath," witches and warlocks gather from many places to report their mischievous deeds, give rewards, perform marriages, and engage in revelry and obscenity of all kinds.

* * *

'Witches and demonologists have long delved into the concept of the devil and evil, illuminating the depths of human darkness and reminding us that true power lies in understanding our fears'

* * *

'Amidst the tales of witches and demonologists lies

the eternal question: Does evil exist solely in the devil or does it reside within us, waiting to be awakened'

* * *

'Knowledge can be transformative, but it is the intent behind its utilisation that determines whether it leads to enlightenment or becomes a dangerous tool in the hands of witches and demonologists, unravelling the complexities of the concept of the devil and evil'

* * *

'Within the realm of witches and demonologies, the concept of the devil and evil serves as a haunting reminder of the delicate balance between darkness and light, binding together the forces that shape our perception of the supernatural'

* * *

'Within the realm of witches and demonologies, the concept of the devil and evil reveals the eternal dance between darkness and light; an exploration of the shadows that ultimately illuminates the strength of the human spirit'

Part 3

Portrayal of the devil & evil in religious texts

Ancient Mythology
Egyptian Mythology
Christianity
Judaism
Hinduism
Buddism
Islam

Chapter 1

Ancient mythology

In ancient mythology, the devil was not just a character of evil, but a reminder for mankind to resist the temptations that lead us astray.

The devil and evil in ancient mythology

Loki in Norse mythology

Evil and its manifestations have always played a significant role in ancient mythology. One prominent figure associated with evil in Norse mythology is Loki. In Norse mythology, Loki is a complex character known for his cunning and mischief. He is known as a shape-shifter, capable of taking various forms to deceive and manipulate others. As such, he embodies the essence of evil and chaos in the Norse pantheon.

Loki is often depicted as a trickster, constantly challenging the order and stability of the gods. His antics create discord and strife among the deities, causing them to question their own identities and alliances. Loki's actions ultimately lead to the downfall of the gods in the Ragnarok, the cataclysmic event that marks the end of the mythical Norse world.

Loki's malevolent nature is also reflected in his role as the father of monstrous creatures such as the giant wolf Fenrir and the world-serpent Jormungandr. These creatures symbolise the destructive forces of nature and the chaos that lurks beneath the surface of the ordered world. Loki's association with these creatures further emphasises his connection to evil and his disruptive influence on the divine realm.

However, it is important to note that Loki's portrayal is not entirely black and white. Despite his villainous actions, Loki also displays moments of bravery and loyalty. For instance, he aids the gods when they are in peril and even sacrifices himself for their sake. This moral ambiguity adds depth to his character and challenges the notion of absolute evil in ancient mythology.

Furthermore, Loki's character serves as a reminder that evil is not always external but can also arise from within. His inclusion in Norse mythology highlights the human capacity for mischief, deception, and betrayal. Through Loki, ancient Norse mythology explores the duality of human nature and the constant struggle between good and evil within each individual.

* * *

In conclusion, Loki's character in Norse mythology represents the embodiment of evil, chaos, and disruption. He challenges the established order and creates discord among the gods. However, his complex nature also offers insights into the human capacity for mischief and betrayal. By examining characters like Loki, we gain a deeper understanding of the complexities of evil in ancient mythology and its relevance in shaping human narratives.

* * *

Chapter 2

Egyptian mythology

'Within Egyptian Mythology, the pursuit of wisdom reminds us the the true conqueror of evil lies in understanding its origins and transforming it through knowledge and enlightenment'

The devil and evil in Egyptian mythology

In Egyptian mythology the devil personifies chaos, deceit, and destruction.

In Egyptian mythology, the concept of evil and the presence of the devil are not as prominent as in other religious beliefs. Instead, the focus is more on the balance between good and evil, and the constant struggle between order and chaos. The ancient Egyptians believed in a variety of gods and goddesses, each with their own roles and responsibilities. These deities represented different aspects of the natural world and often had characteristics that could be both positive and negative.

Set, also known as Seth or Sutekh

One of the most well-known figures in Egyptian mythology is Set, also known as Seth or Sutekh. Set is often seen as a disruptive and chaotic force, associated with storms, turmoil and destruction. However, it is important to note that Set was not necessarily perceived as purely evil. In fact, he was considered an integral part of the world and the natural order. His role as a challenger was seen as necessary for the maintenance of balance.

Demons and spirits that could cause harm to humans

The ancient Egyptians also believed in the existence of demons and spirits that could cause harm to humans. These malevolent beings were often associated with illness, misfortune, and various calamities. However, these evil entities were not seen as ultimate forces of evil, but rather as manifestations of chaos and disorder. The Egyptians believed that by appeasing the gods and performing rituals, they could protect themselves from the influence of these malevolent beings.

The concept of judgment and the afterlife

Another important aspect of Egyptian mythology is the concept of judgment and the afterlife. In the Egyptian belief system, individuals would be judged based on their actions in life and their adherence to ma'at, the principle of order and balance. Those who lived virtuously and upheld ma'at would be rewarded in the afterlife, while those who acted unjustly would face punishment.

* * *

Overall, while the concept of evil and the devil as seen in other religions may not be as prominent in Egyptian mythology, the principle of balance and the struggle between order and chaos is central to their beliefs. The ancient Egyptians recognised the presence of disruptive forces and malevolent beings, but did not attribute them to a single figure of evil. Instead, they emphasised the importance of maintaining harmony and upholding ma'at in order to navigate the complexities of the world and attain spiritual salvation in the afterlife.

* * *

Chapter 3
Christianity

'In the face of darkness, faith in God's goodness shines even brighter, for it is through embracing his light that we conquer the devil's schemes and overcome evil'

The devil and evil in Christianity

While the devil is a prominent figure in Christianity, other religions have their own versions of a malevolent being that embodies evil.

In Christianity, Satan is depicted as a fallen angel who rebelled against God and tempts humanity to sin. The story of Adam and Eve in the Bible's Book of Genesis is a testament to the devil's ability to corrupt the innocence of mankind. This notion of evil serves to emphasise the importance of resisting temptation and following a righteous path.

Christianity, one of the world's largest religions, has always grappled with the concept of evil and the existence of the devil. In Christian theology, evil is seen as a force that battles against the goodness and righteousness of God. The devil, also known as Satan or Lucifer, is traditionally considered the embodiment of evil and the leader of fallen angels who rebelled against God.

Throughout history, the concept of the devil and evil has played a significant role in shaping Christian beliefs and practices. The early Christian church saw evil as a consequence of humanity's disobedience to God, with Adam and Eve's fall from grace leading to the corruption of the world. The devil was seen as the tempter, the one who seduced mankind into sin, and perpetuated evil in the world.

In Christian teachings, the devil is often portrayed as a cunning and deceitful figure who seeks to undermine God's plan and lead people astray. Through lies, deception, and manipulations, the devil tempts individuals into committing acts that are contrary to God's will. This constant struggle between good and evil is at the core of many Christian beliefs and serves as a reminder of the importance of choosing righteousness and resisting temptation.

The devil is often depicted as a fearsome figure, associated with darkness, fire, and suffering. He is believed to rule over hell, a place of eternal punishment for the wicked. However, Christianity also teaches that evil and the devil do not have ultimate power and will ultimately be defeated by God. The victory of good over evil is symbolised in the crucifixion and resurrection of Jesus Christ, who is seen as the saviour of humanity and the conqueror of sin and death.

Despite the profound belief in the existence of evil and the devil, Christianity also emphasises the power of redemption and forgiveness. Christians are encouraged to resist evil and lead lives of righteousness, with the promise of salvation and eternal life in the presence of God. The recognition of the reality of evil serves as a reminder to Christians to remain vigilant, uphold their faith, and seek the guidance and protection of God in their daily lives.

* * *

In conclusion, the concept of evil and the devil in Christianity is a deeply ingrained belief rooted in the narrative of the fall of humanity and the struggle between good and evil. The devil is seen as a powerful force that corrupts and tempts individuals, but ultimately, Christians believe in the eventual triumph of good and God's victory over evil. The recognition of evil serves as a reminder to Christians to stay faithful and live a life in accordance with God's teachings.

* * *

Chapter 4

Judaism

'The true strength of Judaism lies in the unwavering belief that evil exists not as an all-powerful force, but rather as a mere presence that can be overcome through righteous actions and the pursuit of goodness'

The devil and evil in Judaism

The concept of the devil and evil holds great significance in the Jewish community. It is a topic that has been debated and discussed for centuries, and has shaped the beliefs and practices of Judaism. The devil, known as Satan or the adversary, is seen as a powerful and malevolent figure who tempts individuals to sin and opposes God. Evil, on the other hand, is seen as the result of human actions that go against the will of God.

In Jewish theology, the devil is not seen as an independent force, but rather as a servant of God. He is believed to test the faith and righteousness of individuals, as seen in the story of Job in the Hebrew Bible. The devil is portrayed as cunning and deceitful, using various tactics to lead individuals astray from the path of righteousness. However, it is ultimately up to the individual to resist these temptations and choose the path of righteousness.

The concept of evil in Judaism is complex, as it is not seen as an inherent trait, but rather a result of human actions. Judaism believes in the inherent goodness and free will of human beings. It is believed that individuals have the ability to choose between good and evil, and are responsible for their own actions. Evil is seen as the result of human choices that go against the will of God, and is seen as a disruption of the divine plan.

In Jewish tradition, there are various rituals and practices that aim to protect individuals from the influence of the devil and evil. This includes reciting prayers, studying the Torah, and observing the commandments. It is believed that by following these practices, individuals can strengthen their connection with God and resist the temptations of the devil.

The concept of the devil and evil serves as a reminder for individuals to be vigilant and conscious of their actions. It encourages individuals to strive for righteousness and resist the temptations of the devil. By understanding the concept of evil, individuals can better navigate the challenges and complexities of life, and make choices that align with their values and beliefs.

* * *

In conclusion, the concept of the devil and evil holds great significance in the Jewish community. It serves as a reminder for individuals to resist temptation and choose the path of righteousness. By understanding the complexities of evil, individuals can better navigate life and make choices that align with their beliefs and values. The concept of the devil and evil is an integral part of Jewish theology and shapes the beliefs and practices of Judaism.

* * *

Chapter 5
Hinduism

'In Hinduism, the true battle lies not in fighting external evil forces, but in conquering the darkness within oneself'

The devil and evil in Hinduism

In Hinduism, there is the concept of Asuras, powerful supernatural beings who represent chaos and oppose the divine order.

The concept of Asuras

In Hinduism, the concept of Asuras holds great significance. Asuras are often depicted as powerful, supernatural beings who are associated with negativity and evil. They are considered to be the opponents of the Devas, or gods, and are constantly engaged in a cosmic battle with them.

According to Hindu mythology, Asuras were originally born from the breath of Brahma, the creator of the universe. However, their nature and behaviour soon began to deviate from the path of righteousness, causing them to be labeled as "demonic" beings. Asuras are often portrayed as being driven by their desires and ego, which leads them to commit various acts of aggression and violence.

One of the most famous Asuras in Hindu mythology is Ravana, the antagonist in the epic Ramayana. Ravana, the king of Lanka, is notorious for his arrogance and lust for power. His desire to possess Sita, the wife of Lord Rama, leads to his downfall and eventual death. Ravana's story serves as a cautionary tale, warning believers of the consequences of succumbing to their inner demons.

While Asuras are commonly associated with negativity, it is important to note that they are not inherently evil. In fact, many Asuras possess great intelligence and incredible powers. Some Asuras were even respected figures in ancient Indian society, known for their wisdom and knowledge.

The concept of Asuras serves as a representation of the eternal struggle between good and evil, light and darkness. It reminds believers that one must constantly strive to overcome their inner Asuras and embrace the path of righteousness. By conquering their desires and ego, individuals can ultimately attain spiritual liberation.

In Hinduism, the focus is not on outright banishing or eradicating the Asuras, but rather on achieving a balance between the positive and negative forces within oneself. This balance is believed to be crucial for personal growth and spiritual enlightenment.

* * *

In conclusion, the concept of Asuras in Hinduism serves as a reminder of the eternal struggle between good and evil. They symbolise the negative tendencies within individuals and the importance of overcoming these qualities in order to achieve spiritual liberation. By embracing the teachings of Hinduism, believers strive to find the balance between light and darkness, ultimately attaining self-transformation and spiritual enlightenment.

* * *

Chapter 6
Buddism

'The greatest victory over the devil and evil is not in conquering them, but in transcending their presence through inner peace and enlightenment'

The devil and evil in Buddhism

In Buddhism, Mara is seen as a tempter and embodiment of desire, leading individuals astray from enlightenment.

Mara: The tempter and embodiment of desire

Mara, in Buddhism, is a concept that represents desire, attachment, and the delusion of the self. It is often depicted as a demon or tempter who seduces individuals away from the path of enlightenment. The idea of Mara serves as a powerful metaphor for the challenges and obstacles we face in our pursuit of spiritual liberation.

In Buddhist philosophy, the ultimate goal is to attain nirvana, a state of complete liberation from suffering and the cycle of rebirth. However, the journey towards nirvana is not an easy one; it requires discipline, self-control, and the ability to overcome the temptations and distractions of the world.

Mara symbolises the external and internal forces that hinder our progress on the spiritual path. Externally, Mara represents the distractions and allurements of the physical world, such as material possessions, pleasure, and power. These temptations can lead us astray and keep us locked in the cycle of desire and suffering.

Internally, Mara represents our own inner demons – our fears, doubts, and negative emotions. These internal obstacles can create self-doubt, attachment to the ego, and a sense of separation from others. Mara represents the delusions and illusions that cloud our minds, preventing us from seeing the true nature of reality.

To conquer Mara, one must develop mindfulness and insight. Mindfulness allows us to observe and recognise the presence of Mara in our lives – the desires, attachments, and negative thoughts that arise. With insight, we can understand the impermanent and empty nature of these phenomena, realising that they are not essential to our well-being or happiness.

The concept of Mara also teaches us the importance of compassion and interconnectedness. By recognising that all beings are subject to the influence of Mara, we can develop empathy and understanding towards others. Rather than seeing them as enemies or obstacles, we can approach them with kindness and support, recognising that they, too, are on their own journey towards liberation.

* * *

In conclusion, the concept of Mara in Buddhism serves as a powerful metaphor for the challenges we face in our spiritual journey. It reminds us of the temptations and distractions of the physical world and the inner obstacles of desire, attachment, and delusion. By developing mindfulness, insight, and compassion, we can conquer Mara and move closer towards the ultimate goal of liberation.

* * *

Chapter 7
Islam

'In the face of evil, Islam teaches us to strengthen our faith and seek refuge in the mercy of Allah, for darkness cannot triumph in the presence of the almighty'

The devil and evil in Islam

In Islam, the devil, known as Iblis or Shaytan, plays a significant role in tempting and misleading humans away from the righteous path.

The concept of Iblis or Shaytan

The concept of Iblis or Shaytan holds significant importance in Islam and plays a crucial role in the belief system of Muslims. Iblis, also known as Satan, is considered to be a malevolent creature who refused to bow down to Adam and was banished from the presence of Allah.

According to Islamic teachings, Iblis was once among the angels and was regarded as one of the most pious. However, his arrogance and disobedience led to his downfall and eternal condemnation. It is believed that Iblis was filled with envy when Allah created Adam and commanded the angels to bow down before him. Iblis, being filled with pride, refused to bow down, arguing that he was far superior to Adam as he was created from fire while Adam was created from clay.

Allah, in his infinite wisdom, banished Iblis from paradise and cursed him for eternity. Iblis, consumed by his anger and resentment, swore to mislead humankind from the path of righteousness and obedience to Allah. He became the epitome of evil and a constant adversary to human beings.

In Islamic tradition, the concept of Iblis serves as a warning to believers about the dangers of arrogance, disobedience, and the importance of humility and submission to Allah. Muslims are encouraged to seek refuge in Allah from the whispers and temptations of Iblis, and to constantly strive to resist his influence.

The story of Iblis also highlights the concept of free will in Islam. Unlike angels who are created to obey Allah without question, human beings have been granted free will, allowing them to choose between good and evil. Iblis serves as a constant test for believers, as he tries to lure them away from the path of righteousness through deception and temptation.

However, it is important to note that while Iblis may tempt humans, he does not have the power to force them to commit evil acts. Ultimately, it is the responsibility of each individual to resist his influence and make choices that align with the teachings of Islam.

* * *

In conclusion, the concept of Iblis or Shaytan in Islam represents the embodiment of evil and serves as a constant test for believers. Through the story of Iblis, Muslims are reminded of the dangers of arrogance, disobedience, and the importance of staying steadfast in their faith. It is through the constant struggle against the whispers of Iblis that believers can strengthen their relationship with Allah and strive for righteousness.

* * *

Part 4
Evidence of demonic possession in our world today

Quantz (1994)

"Clifford N. R. Quantz's dissertation emerged out of a sincere desire to find answers to the physical, emotional, and spiritual bondage that plagued Christians. After many years of pastoral ministry, he was convinced that something was not complete in his ministry and he wanted to help these troubled people. At the end of his dissertation he came to the conclusion that Satan and his evil spirits do hinder Christians today with various degrees of bondage due to personal and generational sins and covenants. The data for this conclusion is found in case studies, the biblical data and the present-day experiences of other counsellors"

Chapter 1

Cases of demonic possession throughout history

'In the digital age, one can't help but wonder if demonic possession is the work of evil spirits or simply the toxicity of online negativity taking hold of vulnerable souls'

Demonic possession, a phenomenon that has intrigued humanity for centuries, continues to raise questions about the supernatural and the existence of evil forces beyond our realm. While skeptics may dismiss the concept as mere superstition, there have been several documented cases throughout history that defy rational explanation and force us to reconsider our understanding of the spiritual world.

The Loudun Possessions - France - 17th Century

One such case occurred in the early 17th century in France, known as the Loudun Possessions. It involved a group of nuns who exhibited bizarre behaviour, including convulsions, speaking in tongues, and levitation. The local authorities, believing these actions to be the work of Satan, turned to exorcism as a means to alleviate the nuns' suffering. Famed exorcist Father Urbain Grandier was accused of possessing and bewitching the nuns, ultimately leading to his public execution. Despite his death, the possessions continued, leaving experts perplexed and questioning the true nature of these events.

Anneliese Michel, a young German woman in the 1970s

Another well-known case of demonic possession is that of Anneliese Michel, a young German woman in the 1970s. Anneliese's possession manifested through violent outbursts, speaking in different voices, and refusal to consume food or water. Desperate for help, her family turned to the Catholic Church, which approved an exorcism. Unfortunately, Anneliese's condition worsened, and she ultimately lost her life due to malnutrition. The controversial nature of her case sparked public debate and led to the trial of the priests involved in her exorcism.

Clara Germana Cele, a South African girl in the late 20th century

More recent cases of demonic possession have been documented as well, such as that of Clara Germana Cele, a South African girl in the late 20th century. Clara's possession included supernatural strength, a deep aversion to religious symbols, and the ability to understand and speak in languages she had never learned. Numerous witnesses corroborated her extraordinary abilities, leaving many to wonder if a demonic presence had indeed taken control of her.

* * *

While these cases may defy logical explanations, they remind us of the intricacies of the human mind and the unknown depths of the spiritual realm. They challenge our conventional understanding of reality and force us to question whether there are forces beyond our comprehension. Whether one believes in the existence of demonic possession or not, these cases serve as a constant reminder that we have yet to fully grasp the complexities of our world.

* * *

In conclusion, true cases of demonic possession continue to baffle experts and tantalise the human imagination. Whether attributed to mental illness, spiritual forces, or a combination of both, these cases force us to confront the boundaries of our understanding. As we delve deeper into the realms of the unknown, we must approach these phenomena with an open mind and a willingness to explore, not only for the sake of curiosity but also for the possibility of expanding our understanding of the universe in which we live.

* * *

Chapter 2

Case One - James

Quantz (1994)

Background and History

“James was ritualistically abused at a local day-care centre by one man and at least two females. This occurred from the ages of about three through seven years, at which time the abuse was discovered.

The list of abuses James suffered were as follows.

- He was burned with Bic lighters in the palm of his hands, and yet he said he could not see the burn afterwards. Needles were stuck in his upper right thigh (purpose unknown), mom and dad dolls were used as the children were forced to puncture them with needles, as in voodoo.

- He saw the women dressing up as witches and the man as a devil and they would dance around the caldron, which James said looked like a big black "stew pot." Parts of animals were in the pot, and other things that he could not identify. The children were given a drink from a large cup and he did not know what it tasted like except "terrible." One of the attendants told James that Jesus was a "joke.

The parents institutionalised their son because he became threatening at home with such activities as deliberately urinating in the middle of the carpet, and threatening, at times, for no apparent reason to "burn the house down" as he roamed around in the middle of the night.

Conclusion and Observation

From personal observation with James, it seems reasonable to believe that his spiritual, emotional, and physical trauma was directly related to Satanic ritual abuse suffered at the day-care centre.

James improved dramatically in his emotional and mental responses after the demonic influences were eliminated from his life. He was able to sleep better and he ceased threatening to burn down the house. In the fall of that year, he was enrolled again in the public-school system and his grades increased substantially. He had never been involved much in "rough and tumble" sports prior to this time, but now wanted to play football.

The case of James would tend to support Clifford N. R. Quantz's hypothesis that Satan can affect the emotional, physical, and spiritual health of individuals. Further, when demons are dealt with on this level, good health in these areas seems to be restored"

* * *

Chapter 3

Case Two - Ben

Quantz (1994)

Background and History

“Ben is a married man in his mid-forties. He is a well-educated professional type, a former junior college professor, and now the head of a company sales department which demands that he travel extensively around the country. Ben has been divorced, and is now married to a clinical nurse specialist. This marriage was in shambles when the case came to my attention, and the couple was separated, with Ben living in another city. Divorce proceedings were considered by his wife, Pam, but had not been initiated as yet due to various reasons, one being that Pam was still hoping against hope that Ben could be changed. Ben loved the life of the "Jet Set," lived above his means in a fantasy world of romance, and was in financial as well as spiritual decline.

Ben had given his heart to Christ as a ninth grader. As a senior in high school he felt a "loud deafening" call to some form of ministry in the church, and applied for credentials at the district meeting of his denomination. It never did go well because Ben sensed that in strange ways he was hindered from fulfilling his calling.

Pam was in touch with many medical professionals, and was trying to find some answers to Ben's bizarre behaviour from them.

Pam was visibly shaken and distraught when she finally called me for an appointment in March 1988. She had decided to try my ministry after she had thoroughly investigated my counselling, In desperation she had decided to go to someone who demonstrated a knowledge of spiritual warfare, but could not find satisfaction in her own parish leadership. Even though her formal high church background gave her considerable reasons to have reservations about such proceedings, she grasped at the only remaining hope she could see. From that day onward, she began attending our newly established church and came into a vital relationship with Jesus Christ as her personal Saviour. Pam was soon to become a good friend of my wife, and this friendship developed over the subsequent months as Pam leaned heavily upon my wife in those days of crisis.

Pam persuaded a somewhat reluctant husband to come and meet with me about their need. He consented to do so, and one strong incentive was to get back into his home again. However, the vibes he was sending out were confusing.

Conclusion and Observation

Our struggles to get Ben free in Christ were long and hard.

There were times when I was not sure I could keep on paying the price in time and emotional energy. However, we did continue in the struggle and saw a life, a home, and a family restored in Christ.

Ben and Pam are members of our church and take an active part in teaching and in other areas of service. It is quite obvious that Satan had challenged God's claim upon Ben, and did his best to take him away from Christ's kingdom, even when it first appeared that Ben wanted to serve Christ in full-time Christian service. The 'mark' witnessed by the evil spirits I interpreted to be the mark of Christ's sovereign choice"

* * *

Chapter 4

Case Three - Lila

Quantz (1994)

"Lila is a married woman1 in her early thirties who has four children. She lives in Angola, Indiana. She came to my attention through a minister friend who was perplexed by this woman's lack of positive response to conventional medical treatment and counselling therapy, and wondered if I would help her. Her husband was so stressed by Lila's inability to function normally around the home that he was desperate enough to do almost anything within reason.

Lila was a born-again Christian, and attended an evangelical church. Confusion, frustration, and forgetfulness and several medical symptoms were rendering Lila dysfunctional in the normal expectations of family duties.

Conclusion and Observation

Lila's case seems to demonstrate a Christian who had Satanic influences and bondages in her physical, emotional, and spiritual being. Since the physical fatigue miraculously disappeared and Lila now has a bubbling type of energy, one could conclude that evil spirits affected her physically.

Lila has also come alive spiritually in areas which she desperately desired, but could not receive before. Lila and her husband actively help other people in similar circumstances in which they once found themselves. She is truly a vibrant Christian one likes to be around. Further, Lila is now a supervisor trainer at the same job where before she could barely function. A former counsellor, seeing Lila after these sessions, exclaimed: "What has happened to you? You've changed so much I can hardly believe it."

* * *

Part 5

Miscellaneous

Curses

Beware Ouija Boards: opening a portal to the spiritual realm

Why do demons protect their names?

Chapter 1
Curses

'Words have tremendous power, choose them wisely, for curses can haunt and harm long after they are spoken'

Definition of Curses

Quantz (1994)

"Spells and Incantations. Hexes: These are used in witchcraft, voodoo, magic, and sorcery. They involve written or spoken formulas of words and nonsense syllables supposed to be capable of magical effects. The concept stems from the idea that there is a direct relationship between the word spoken and the facts they represent. Sometimes gibberish, or a secret code word, is uttered to hide true meanings from the initiate or victim. The tonal quality is also part of the effectiveness of the spell, curse, or incantation. Some are uttered for protection, others for favours of the person on whom the curse, spell, or incantation is placed (such as the love spell). In a curse, it is meant to harm or even kill. Hexes are sign forms of these curses. The Bible takes cursing and blessing1 seriously, not only when the Lord God is pronouncing them, but also when the evil kingdom of Satan is using them as well. An example is the case of Balaam, where the Lord forbids him to curse the Israelites: He was compelled to pronounce the Lord's blessing instead"

* * *

Curses have been a fascinating and mysterious topic throughout history. Whether it is widely believed or not, the concept of curses exists in various cultures and religions around the world. From ancient times to modern-day, many people have claimed to be victims of curses, experiencing a series of unfortunate events that they attribute to a curse placed upon them. While there is no scientific evidence to support the existence of curses, people continue to seek ways to recognise and cure them.

Recognising a curse can be a challenging task as it often manifests in different forms. Some common signs include a string of bad luck, chronic illness or misfortune, and recurring nightmares or supernatural experiences. However, it is important to note that these signs can also be attributed to natural causes or psychological factors. In some cases, people may genuinely believe they are cursed due to a psychological condition known as the "curse syndrome," where individuals subconsciously convince themselves of their cursed state.

Nevertheless, for those who genuinely believe they are cursed, finding a cure becomes paramount. Various methods have been suggested for lifting curses, ranging from spiritual practices to alternative therapies. In some cultures, rituals involving priests or religious leaders are performed to break the curse. These rituals often involve prayers, incantations, and the use of protective symbols or talismans. Additionally, alternative therapies such as energy healing, crystal therapy, and herbal remedies are also believed to help in removing curses.

However, finding an effective cure for curses requires careful consideration and discernment. It is essential to consult with trusted professionals or practitioners who have expertise in dealing with spiritual matters. These individuals can provide guidance and support through the process of recognising and addressing curses. They can also help differentiate between actual curses and psychological factors, ensuring that the right approach is taken for healing.

Furthermore, it is crucial to maintain a balanced and rational approach when dealing with curses. While belief in curses is a personal choice, it is important to understand that the power of suggestion and the subconscious mind can greatly influence our perception of reality. Therefore, seeking professional help not only provides a clearer perspective but also ensures that appropriate measures are taken to address the underlying issues causing distress.

* * *

In conclusion, curses remain a fascinating and debated topic. While there is no scientific evidence to support their existence, the belief in curses persists in many cultures. Recognising and curing curses require careful examination, consultation with professionals, and a balanced approach. Ultimately, one must navigate the realm of curses with an open mind and the willingness to explore alternative explanations.

* * *

Chapter 2

Beware Ouija Boards: Opening a portal to the spiritual realm

'Be careful not to open doors that are best left closed: the mysteries of the Ouija Board may leave more questions than answers'

Ouija boards have always fascinated and intrigued people around the world. These mystical boards, used as a means of communication with spirits, have both intrigued and scared individuals for generations. Although they are often seen as harmless and used for entertainment purposes, Ouija boards have a long history rooted in the supernatural, offering a gateway to the unknown.

The origins of the Ouija board trace back to the late 19th century when spiritualism was at its peak. Spiritualists believed in the ability to communicate with the spirits of the deceased, and Ouija boards became an essential tool in their practice. The board, adorned with letters, numbers, and a yes or no, acted as an open door to the spiritual realm.

Using a Ouija board involves multiple participants placing their hands on a planchette, a small heart-shaped pointer, and asking questions to the spirits. The planchette then moves across the board, seemingly guided by an unseen force, spelling out answers or messages from the spirits. Many believe that this interaction is facilitated by the energy of the participants and the spirits' desire to communicate.

However, Ouija boards have always evoked a sense of danger and fear. Countless stories and urban legends surround the use of these boards, with claims of summoning malevolent spirits or opening portals to the demonic realm. These tales warn against the potential consequences of tampering with forces beyond our understanding.

Despite the controversy surrounding Ouija boards, many continue to view them as mere entertainment. They are often used at parties or sleepovers, with participants eagerly awaiting messages from the other side. In the hands of skeptics, Ouija boards are dismissed as nothing more than a psychological phenomenon, where the movements of the planchette are influenced by subconscious thoughts and slight hand movements.

Whether one regards Ouija boards as a means of spiritual communication or a harmless game, there is no denying their impact on popular culture and the human fascination with the supernatural. Movies, books, and television shows have all capitalised on the mystique of the Ouija board, further contributing to its allure and intrigue.

* * *

In conclusion, Ouija boards remain a captivating topic, grappling with notions of the unknown and the afterlife. Whether one chooses to indulge in their mysteries or avoid them altogether, Ouija boards will continue to hold a place in the human imagination, offering a tantalising glimpse into the world beyond our perception. Just remember, when encountering the Ouija board, tread carefully, as it may open doors that one cannot easily close.

* * *

Chapter 3

Why demons protect their names?

'Demons protect their names like armour because their power lies in the fear and reverence invoked by their true identity'

In many mythologies and folklore, demons are often depicted as powerful and malevolent beings who possess supernatural abilities and are known for causing harm and chaos. One common characteristic that demons share across various cultures and traditions is their protective nature towards their names. But why do demons place such importance on safeguarding their names?

Firstly, the concept of a name holds significant power and significance in many belief systems. It is believed that knowing a demon's true name grants humans control over them or the ability to summon and manipulate them. By protecting their names, demons aim to maintain their autonomy and prevent others from gaining power over them. Demonic entities are often portrayed as prideful and fiercely independent beings, and relinquishing control to humans would be seen as a sign of weakness.

Secondly, demons may protect their names to preserve their reputation and image. Throughout history, demons have been associated with dark and malevolent forces, and their names have become synonymous with evil. By keeping their names hidden or secret, demons are able to maintain a sense of mystique and fear. Their names become shrouded in secrecy, adding to their aura of power and unpredictability.

Additionally, demons may protect their names to avoid being summoned or banished by those who have knowledge of their true identities. In various occult practices, individuals invoke demons by calling out their names or using specific rituals. By concealing their names, demons can prevent unauthorised summoning or manipulation, ensuring that they remain free to carry out their own agendas without interference.

Furthermore, some legends suggest that knowing a demon's name allows individuals to exert control over them, effectively trapping them or compelling them to carry out specific tasks. By keeping their names hidden, demons safeguard themselves from being captured or coerced into servitude.

In conclusion, demons protect their names for several reasons, including preserving their autonomy, maintaining their reputation, avoiding unwanted summoning, and preventing manipulation or control by humans. The secrecy surrounding their names adds to their perceived power and enhances the fear and awe associated with these malevolent entities. The legends and stories surrounding demons and their names continue to captivate our imaginations, reminding us of the enduring fascination with the supernatural and the unknown.

Names of demons

The world of mythology is filled with various mystical creatures, from gods and goddesses to creatures of darkness. Among these creatures, demons hold a special place. Demons are often depicted as malevolent beings, capable of causing destruction and chaos. These creatures come in different forms and names in various mythologies across the world.

In Indian mythology, there are several well-known demons. One of the most famous demons is Ravana, the antagonist in the epic Ramayana. Ravana, with his ten heads and immense power, symbolises the ultimate evil. Despite his evil nature, Ravana is also portrayed as a learned scholar and a devoted worshipper of Lord Shiva, adding complexities to his character.

Another prominent demon in Indian mythology is Mahishasura, who was eventually defeated by Goddess Durga. Mahishasura was a shape-shifting demon who possessed the ability to transform into different animals. It was only through the combined power of various Hindu gods and goddesses that Mahishasura was vanquished.

In ancient Mesopotamian mythology, Pazuzu was a demon associated with wind and storms. Pazuzu was often depicted as a grotesque creature with wings, a lion or dog-like face, and talons. He was believed to bring famine and disease and was often invoked to ward off other evil spirits.

One of the most infamous demons in Christian theology is Satan. Known as the embodiment of evil, Satan is believed to have rebelled against God and was cast out of heaven. Satan tempts and corrupts human beings, leading them into sin. In literature and popular culture, Satan is often portrayed as a cunning and charismatic figure.

In Japanese mythology, there are several demons, or yokai, which are believed to haunt and torment humans. One such demon is the Oni, a fearsome creature with horns, sharp claws, and a demonic appearance. Oni are often depicted as punishers of evil deeds, but they can also cause harm to humans if crossed.

* * *

In conclusion, demons have a prominent place in mythology across different cultures. Whether it is the powerful and complex characters from Indian mythology, the malevolent creatures from Mesopotamian and Japanese folklore, or the embodiment of evil in Christian theology, demons continue to captivate our imaginations. These creatures symbolize the eternal struggle between good and evil, reminding us of the potential darkness that resides within humanity.

* * *

Call to Action against evil

In conclusion, examining the existence of evil in our modern world is not a passive exercise but a call to action. It requires us to confront the presence of evil within ourselves and in society, and to actively work towards creating a more just and compassionate world.

By taking responsibility for our own actions and choices, we contribute to the eradication of evil in our own lives. This involves developing a strong moral compass that guides our decisions and leads us towards virtuous choices.

But it doesn't stop there. We must also stand up against injustice, advocate for the oppressed, and promote positive change in our communities. This means actively opposing the influence of evil and working towards the creation of a more just society.

By cultivating qualities such as empathy, kindness, and forgiveness, we become agents of positive transformation. We become resilient, compassionate, and enlightened individuals who sow the seeds of a better world for ourselves and future generations.

So let us not simply analyse evil from a distance, but let us actively confront it and take impactful action. Together, we can make a difference and create a world that is free from the shackles of evil.

* * *

Terminology

Within the ethical domain, where righteousness prevails over wickedness, there exists an abundance of words that can cause confusion. In this dedicated section on vocabulary, we have made diligent efforts to encapsulate important terms. It is important to note that these terminologies predominantly originate from a Christian perspective.

Quantz (1994)

Abyss: What we know about the abyss has its basis in the biblical accounts referring to some form of abode for evil spirits. It is mentioned once in Luke 8:31, and the other eight times in the book of Revelation. Evil spirits were afraid of being sent there by Jesus in the case of the Gadarene demoniac, and pleaded with Jesus not to send them there before their time. In the book of Revelation the abyss is mentioned in connection with some end-time onslaught of the spirits released from it in order to torment the people on the earth who have the mark of the beast (Rev 9). It is the place where Satan is cast at the beginning of the one-thousand-year reign of Christ, and is later thrown into the lake of fire (Rev 20:7). The Lord has instructed that these spirits be sent to the abyss. This has been affirmed by the Holy Spirit, as well as the evil spirits, after they are defeated in encounters by the power of Christ.

Amulets: A charm worn as a necklace, bracelet, or anklet among mainly primitive peoples to ward off evil spirits and curses. They usually consist of stones, teeth, claws, or shells. Some modern-day "charms" may fall into this category.

Blasphemy: The general understanding is that blasphemy consists of impious, defiant, and slanderous utterances or actions against the Lord God. For example, the Pharisees who were the guardians of the Scriptures, the temple and its service, could not recognise the Christ, while professing to worship, praise, and exhault the Creator. To call Jesus demon possessed is the epitome of blasphemy.

Blood Pacts: A covenant between two people and/or the devil signed with the letting of blood. These pacts are often made in exchange for protection or special "blessings" from Satan, often involving the promise to sell one's soul for such favours. It sometimes involves drinking blood in some ritual. These must be broken in order for the counselee to be released spiritually and emotionally. Then the blood of Christ needs to be pleaded to cancel the affects on the person's life.

Ceremonies: This seems to be a catch-all term describing special acts of "worship" prayers, incantations, and curses conducted by the coven members to invoke power from the kingdom of Satan in order to carry out their acts of hindrance upon the Lord's cause, and thus gain status and praise from their masters.

Covens: Wiccan groups of usually thirteen individuals who meet secretly for special rites, sacrifices (human and animal), and ceremonies to invoke the power of spirits or Satan. Meeting places are in varied locations such as remote fields, streams, clearings in woods, secret underground tunnels, and even church basements at midnight.

Curses. Spells and Incantations. Hexes: These are used in witchcraft, voodoo, magic, and sorcery. They involve written or spoken formulas of words and nonsense syllables supposed to be capable of magical effects. The concept stems from the idea that there is a direct relationship between the word spoken and the facts they represent. Sometimes gibberish, or a secret code word, is uttered to hide true meanings from the initiate or victim. Some are uttered for protection, others for favours of the person on whom the curse, spell, or incantation is placed (such as the love spell). In a curse, it is meant to harm or even kill. Hexes are sign forms of these curses. The

Bible takes cursing and blessing1 seriously, not only when the Lord God is pronouncing them, but also when the evil kingdom of Satan is using them as well. An example is the case of Balaam, where the Lord forbids him to curse the Israelites: He was compelled to pronounce the Lord's blessing instead.

Demonised: This term is understood to include everything from full possession (Gadarene, Mark 5) to harmful hindrances on the body and mind, and to a lesser extent the general field of harassing access to the psyche of Christians as well as the ungodly.

Esoteric Language: The use of terminology that is known only to the special few. This is common in occult circles, and even common religious terms are employed backwards (like dog for god). When known terms are employed, they are used with entirely opposite meanings, such as "Praise to Jesus" in a counterfeit gift of tongues which can mean "curse Jesus and praise be to god Satan." Sometimes these take the form of nonsense syllables.

ESP and Clairvoyance: Extrasensory perception, extrasensory apparitions, and clairvoyance have to do with a special ability to see and know what others cannot see with the natural eye or through natural channels. These may well be Satan's counterfeiting of the spiritual gifts of prophecy and discernment.

Exorcism: An exorcism carries a connotation of sending out demons. It is the religious or spiritual practice of evicting demons, jinns, or other malevolent spiritual entities from a person, or an area, that is believed to be possessed.

Falsifying or Counterfeiting Gifts: Quantz (1994) believes that Satan engages in counterfeiting the true gifts of the Holy Spirit. One example is false tongues: here an esoteric language is used to veil the cursing and blasphemy against the Lord Jesus. This has been witnessed when testing some people with this false gift. It has been recognised that the spirit responsible for the tongue, when confronted with the power of the Holy Spirit, turns to cursing for discovering him, much to the shock of the persons involved. "Jesus be cursed" (I Cor 12:3).

Incubi and Succubae: In religious terms, this has to do with spook phenomena associated with sexual experiences, especially at night. Individuals have testified to having been somehow held down by a non-physical presence and then sexually assaulted by an unseen presence leaving the victim helpless to defend her/himself. The Jewish tradition of the Lilith speaks of these demons of the night. The victims are often awake or are awakened during these experiences.

Magic: Black and white magic according to some observers can be recognised in three forms: (1) the slight of hand magic of natural causes or circumstances, (2) religious magic, though condemned in the Bible, which employs Bible formulas or words to evoke healing and other effects, and (3) magic or unseen help of demons or the devil to get a desired effect or answer to a need using magic incantations. These are commonly employed to remove warts by magic formulas and are a form of magic healing. The idea of black magic being bad or evil and white magic being good exists only in the minds of the participants, since intended purposes and means are questionable.

Medium/Mediumistic: A person who communicates with spirits of the dead for purposes of advice and information. This is not to construe or identify with those who confront evil spirits as Christ did, in order to identify them and get rid of them. King Saul in the Bible consulted the medium at Endor to his final destruction. In the New Age, this is the movement called channeling.

Mind Control: In popular usage this implies the control of the mind of someone else by "brain washing," or the use of drugs, or any other means to prevent the victim from the free usage of his or her own mind. It has been observed that a form of evil spirit mind control in counselees who testify to not being able, at times, to have any control of their thinking.

Misuse of Divine Names: Quantz (1994) encountered in his research the use of divine names for purposes other than they were intended in the Bible. For example "god" can be used to refer to Satan, or "dog" as a backward form of cursing God Almighty.

False holy ghosts, Jesus, Lord, and other divine names are subtly interchanged with the true in order to deceive the unsuspecting hearers. The magic use of scriptural texts for healing, and the saying of the Lord's prayer backwards, are in Satan's bag of tricks.

Occult: From the Latin "occultus," meaning dark or secret. It usually involves two areas of emphasis: the secret knowledge of things prohibited by God or unknown to man in general, as demonstrated in the first temptation with Eve in the garden of Eden (Gen 3:5), and the use of that power to manipulate or control others or things.

Parapsychology: This started with the Society for Psychical Research in 1882 in England. Members are psychologists and psychiatrists who study the paranormal or spiritistic phenomena. They experiment with spiritistic seances and mediums in order to study firsthand the powers and phenomena behind such things. This is forbidden in the word of God.

Poltergeist or Ghost Apparition: The audio manifestations of spirit entities often mistakenly understood as human spirits. In German, poltergeist means a "rattling ghost," and includes the movement of objects about the room as well.

Rod and Pendulum: One form is water witching to determine the location of water. Some would explain these phenomena as merely playing the magnetic fields of the earth, but it is occult, for when it is prayed against, the ability ceases: It is also used in spiritistic practices when there is the magnetic pendulum to divine answers, thus invoking the help of spirits.

Sacrifices: These refer specifically to animal and human sacrifices made in the worship of Satan to release power, to gain special favours, and to accomplish devilish affects upon God's people. It is believed sacrifices appear to be a form of mockery against the sacrifice of Christ.

Satanic Ritual Abuse and Ritualistic Abuse (SRA): With the media coverage in recent years, this term has been popularised to mean any systematic physical, emotional, and spiritual abuse of a victim, especially children, and emotionally unstable youth and adults. Abuse includes sexual rituals and torture.

Sequelae: Abnormal conditions in a person because of previous abuse, as in Satanic cult ritual abuse, affects and effects, symptoms.

Shamanism: A belief and practice of medicine men or a Shaman, acting as both priest and doctor, engaging powerful spirits to effect cures, spells, and curses.

Signs and Symbols: The occult world employs many power, hex, cursing, and blessing symbols in its nefarious craft of deceit. The list is seemingly unending if one peruses the occult literature. Many Christians unwittingly fall victim to these symbols in literature, toys, and numerous other "innocent" materials foisted upon society by the media. An example is a toy-like form of the Ouiji board placed by a cereal company in its boxes.

Sorcery: The classical definition of sorcery has to do with the supernatural powers exercised by a witch or sorcerer who engages the help of evil spirits.

Sorcery "Religious" and "Ancestral": The definition of sorcery is the art, practices, or spells and powers of a person who is employing the power of evil spirits. There is a great difference of opinion as to power sources, because much is so secret that even those practicing such do not know the reasons why they work. It is believed that this power is from the evil kingdom of Satan. Further, since all power in the universe and beyond centres in Christ, the Holy Spirit, and the Everlasting Father, this strange power of sorcery, witchcraft, or voodoo is a perversion of the divine power given to these angels before they fell from their positions around God's throne. Thus the power is in the spirit realm. Primarily, two forms of sorcery have been distinguished that have been confronted on a regular basis: religious and ancestral.

Religious sorcery has to do with perverting all gospel truth and making it plausible to mankind by hidden meanings behind sacred words and power displayed in perverted rituals. This is the essence of spiritual Babylon that leads the whole world astray, as revealed in the book of Revelation. Ancestral sorcery is that passed down through the generational lines.

Talisman: An inanimate object supposed to possess a supernatural capacity of imparting special blessings in contrast to the amulet that is supposed to ward off evil. The talisman usually consists of a disc of stone or metal on which is engraved astrological, magical, or occult symbols.

Trance State: Likened to the catatonic state in psychiatry, the person seems to be oblivious to any of his or her surroundings, and sits motionless and often staring into nothingness. This condition has been observed in people with a dumb, cursed, or trance spirit in their persons. The same people confessed after coming out of the catatonic state that they were under such demon control that even though they were yelling inside, the spirit would not let them speak. They could do nothing until the counsellors drove out that spirit.

Transfer of Spirits: Dr. Ralph Allison tells of his experiences in his psychiatric practice of these other entities or personalities passing from one person to another. His observations are correct to an extent in that these foreign entities are passing from one person to another, but they may be evil spirits when the conditions are correct, because of legal grounds or by invitation.

New Age channeling comes into this category even though the New Agers claim them to be benevolent spirit guides. Not only do these evil spirits move at will or by command from those higher up in the demonic hierarchy, they can be moved by the power of Christ and the Holy Spirit in order to be confronted and expelled. This has been witnessed often in the deliverance group among the intercessors.

Witchcraft: The practice of magic arts using potions, unguents, powders, sacrifices, and blood to cast spells and gain favours with the help of evil spirits. Witches are female and warlocks are considered male. On their "Sabbath," witches and warlocks gather from many places to report their mischievous deeds, give rewards, perform marriages, and engage in revelry and obscenity of all kinds.

Meet the Author - Wendy Sheffield

From a young age, the author has been acutely aware of the perpetual battle between good and evil. It was through the captivating realm of horror movies that her fascination with the dark side first took hold, as it does for many. As special effects evolved in these movies, so did the intricacies of their storylines, provoking contemplation about the essence of existence itself.

While most people might not take the devil and evil as depicted in films seriously, the author did. Although she couldn't fully comprehend her early intrigue, her growing understanding of spirituality made it clear that she needed to acquaint herself with both good and evil to safeguard herself and help others appreciate that knowledge is a potent force. She recognised that one cannot simply disregard unpleasant aspects.

By the time readers conclude this book, she hopes that they will no longer be afraid of life's darker aspects. Instead, she desires for them to awaken each morning bathed in light, knowing they are aligned with what is right!

* * *

facebook.com/spiritwriterspeaks
instagram.com/healingwithspirit.co.uk
youtube.com/healingwithspirit7965

Bibliography

Quantz, Clifford N.R., "An Investigation of Satanic Influences Upon Physically, Emotionally, and Spiritually Disturbed Christians: Selected Case Studies" (1994). Professional Dissertations DMin. 616. https://dx.doi.org/10.32597/dmin/616 https://digitalcommons.andrews.edu/dmin/616

Printed in Great Britain
by Amazon

39463021R00076